Mrs. Twiggenbotham Goes to Town

To Jamie and Ryan,
Two Very Precious Grandsons

For God has made them so.

Mrs. Twiggenbotham Goes to Town

© 2003 by Emily King

Published by Kregel Kidzone, an imprint of Kregel Publications, P.O. Box 2607, Grand Rapids, MI 49501.

For more information about Kregel Publications, visit our Web site: www.kregel.com.

ISBN 0-8254-3064-X

Printed in South Korea
03 04 05 06 / 4 3 2 1

Mrs. Twiggenbotham Goes to Town

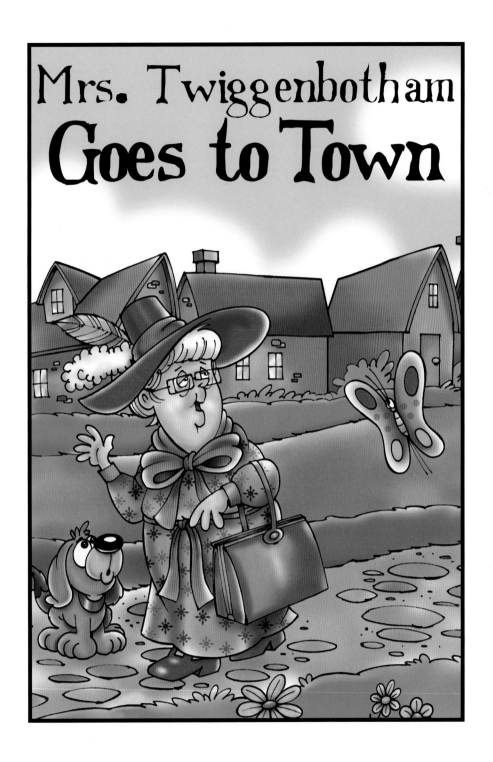

Written by **Emily King**

Illustrated by **Rick Incrocci**

In the cozy town of Smithville, Mrs. Twiggenbotham woke one fine spring morning.

"What a lovely day," she said out loud. "Thank you, God, for this day."

Now, it didn't matter whether the sun shone or the rain pitter-pattered on her bedroom window. Mrs. Twiggenbotham considered every day a lovely day because God had made it so.

Before she got out of bed, she put on her spectacles, which were as thick as pop-bottle bottoms. You see, Mrs. Twiggenbotham couldn't see very well. In fact, even with her glasses perched perfectly on her nose, she still couldn't see very far. But what she saw gave her pleasure, because God had made it so.

"I think I'll go to town this morning," she said to her fluffy white cat, Lily. Lily watched as Mrs. Twiggenbotham chose a pretty patterned dress and slipped into her shoes. She wore red shoes because they were easier to find when she wanted to go somewhere in a hurry. On her head she plopped a fancy hat with a feather on the side, and kissed her dear little kitty good-bye.

"Good morning, Mr. Crumpacker," she said to her neighbor's lamppost. "Hmmm. He must have laryngitis," she said when she got no response. "I'll pray for your quick recovery, Mr. Crumpacker," she said.

The Smithville bus rumbled to the curb and wheezed its doors open.

"Good morning, Miss Partridge," Mrs. Twiggenbotham said to the driver. "I've brought you some plum conserve." She dug in her bag, clanking and jingling the contents, and found a small jar filled with deep purple jam.

"Why, thank you," said Miss Partridge. "I think plums are very tasty."

"Yes, I think so too," said Mrs. Twiggenbotham. "How wonderful of God to make them so."

She eased into a front bench seat that felt unusually lumpy.

"Good morning, Mrs. Twiggenbotham," said Mr. Binklesworth from under her.

"Oh, my word!" she sputtered. "Oh, Mr. Binklesworth, pardon me," she said, scooting down beside him.

"No harm done," he chuckled. He knew that even with her glasses perched perfectly on her nose, she still couldn't see very far.

"You are most gracious," she replied. "Now tell me about your grandson off at college."

The bus bumped merrily along, through the narrow lanes, past cottages and flower gardens, until it came to Main Street in the heart of Smithville. Mrs. Twiggenbotham got off and set about visiting the quaint little shops.

She entered the antique shop owned by Harry Hildenthorpe. Velvet chairs and cherrywood tables, china teacups and crystal bowls filled every nook and cranny. Even a person with excellent eyesight had to watch for breakables while getting through the maze of tiny aisles.

"Yoo-hoo, Mr. Hildenthorpe," she yodeled.

Harry Hildenthorpe emerged from the back room. "Hello, Mrs. Twiggenbotham. What can I do for you this beautiful day?"

"Well, I want to buy a gift for my niece, Penelope. I'd like something lovely and delicate."

As she spoke, she felt her way along, peering at the shiny things that caught her attention.

"Here is something pretty," she said. "A crystal vase. Penelope loves flowers. I think she'll like this to display them on her . . . Oh . . . what a nice oil lamp. But, no, I think she'd like the vase better, thank you."

Pleased with her purchase, she headed toward the candy store across the street. On her way, she heard the groan of a road-painting machine. It left a yellow trail down the middle of Main Street, like a slug depositing its shiny path behind it. She knew Serafina Swathmore drove the rig.

"Oh, Serafina," Mrs. Twiggenbotham called, "I'm so glad I ran into you. I have something for you." She dug in her big red bag, clanking and jingling the contents, and drew out a scarf knitted in all the colors of the rainbow.

"I made this for you to wear on damp, chilly mornings. The rainbow colors will remind you of God's promise and his love."

"How thoughtful of you. Thank you so much." Serafina hung the scarf around her neck.

"And I wondered, Serafina, would you like to come after church on Sunday for sausages and sauerkraut?"

"Oh, I'd love to, Mrs. Twiggenbotham," Serafina answered.

"Now, now, I mustn't keep you," the old woman said and ambled again toward the candy store, leaving yellow Twiggenbotham-shaped footprints in the street.

"I'll have some of that licorice," she said, pointing to the black twisted vines. "And some sour lemon drops for Mr. Crumpacker. Touch of laryngitis, poor dear."

She stuffed two white bags into her purse beside the purple bag with the vase for Penelope. "Good day, and God bless you," she said to Mandy Magurk, whom the children of Smithville called Mandy the Candy Lady.

She stopped at the yarn shop and bought another rainbow-colored skein of wool and a bright pink skein for her cat.

"My dear Lily loves to play with yarn," she said to Clara Klingenberry, the shop owner.

"Oh, I know, I know," said Clara. "I have two kitties myself, and yarn balls are their favorite toys. I think cats are among the most graceful of animals, don't you?"

"Oh, surely they are," said Mrs. Twiggenbotham, "for God has made them so."

The church bells chimed noon.

"Oh, my word, noon already," she said. "I must be off. Good day, Clara, and God bless you."

When she whipped around, her purse just missed a mountain of neatly piled skeins. Mrs. Klingenberry shook her head and smiled. She knew that even with her glasses perched perfectly on her nose, her friend couldn't see very far.

Mrs. Twiggenbotham hustled to the tiny Smithville church at the end of the street. A heavy wooden door closed behind her. Quiet wrapped her in its peaceful arms, as if someone had shushed the world. Sunshine beamed through large, leaded-glass panes and splashed their colors on the walls.

Mrs. Twiggenbotham knew this church as well as her own home. She shuffled down the carpeted aisle and knocked on the side door.

Pastor Potter grinned, and his blue eyes twinkled under snowy eyebrows when he saw her. "Why, Mrs. Twiggenbotham. How nice to see you. And what brings you here on this fine day?"

She dug in her bag as she spoke. "Well, Pastor, I thought I'd make you and Mrs. Potter a loaf of my lemon-blueberry tea bread. I remembered how you enjoyed it at the church potluck."

"How sweet of you," he said. "Would you like to stay and have some with us?"

"Thank you, Pastor," she said, "but I must be on my way. I've got one more stop to make before I ride the bus home. Give my love to Pearl. Good day, and God bless you."

"And God bless you, Mrs. Twiggenbotham," he said.

"Oh, he has, in many, many ways," she said with a smile almost as bright as the sunshine.

A tiny bell jingled overhead as Mrs. Twiggenbotham entered Bernard Butterby's butcher shop.

Even Mrs. Twiggenbotham could see that Mr. Butterby's chin hung sadly on his chest. His shoulders drooped like lettuce wilting in the summer sun.

You see, Mr. Butterby's best friend had moved far away to lead safaris in the deepest parts of Africa.

"I know what Bernard needs," Mrs. Twiggenbotham had said to herself. "A good dose of God's love!"

"Lord," she prayed, "show your love through me."

"Hello, Mrs. Twiggenbotham," Mr. Butterby sighed. "What can I get for you today?"

"Well, I'll have some liver for Lily and six plump sausages," she said.

He handed her two neat bundles wrapped in butcher paper. "Will there be anything else?"

"As a matter of fact, there is," she said, setting her purse on the counter. She removed this bag and that one, until she found a round cookie tin.

"Here, Mr. Butterby. I've made you some coconut cookies to have with your tea."

For the first time in a long time, Bernard's frown turned upside-down. "Why, Mrs. Twiggenbotham, how did you know?"

"How did I know what, dear?" she asked.

"How did you know that these are my very favorite cookies? My sweet mother used to make these for me when I was having a bad day. What a coincidence," he chuckled.

"I'm so glad you like them," she said, "but I do not believe in coincidences. I believe in God-incidents. And I believe God wanted you to taste his love in these cookies. He just worked through me, that's all."

She stuffed her bags back into her purse. "Well, I must catch the bus for home. I wonder, will you be free for lunch Sunday afternoon? I'm having some friends over for sausages and sauerkraut."

"Yes, I . . . I'd love that," Bernard answered.

"Wonderful, wonderful," she replied. "We'll see you about one o'clock then. Good day. And God bless you, Mr. Butterby."

Mrs. Twiggenbotham toted her very heavy bag to the bus stop. As the bus bustled down Main Street, she waved.

Although Mrs. Twiggenbotham didn't know it, Mr. Hildenthorpe, Miss Swathmore, Miss Magurk, Mrs. Klingenberry, Pastor Potter, and Mr. Butterby all waved back. They knew that even with her glasses perched perfectly on her nose, Mrs. Twiggenbotham still couldn't see very far. But they also knew that she had the biggest heart in all of Smithville.

For God had made it so.

Mrs. Twiggenbotham's Plum Conserve
Makes 3 ½ cups
This makes enough to have some to share with your neighbors.
You can eat it like jam on toast or crackers, or try it warm on
chicken or fish.

1 ½ pounds plums (3 cups cut up)
1 orange (juice and grated rind*)
¾ cup raisins

2 cups sugar
½ cup chopped walnuts

1. Wash plums, remove pits. Cut up into chunks and place in a medium pot.

2. Grate the rind of the orange and squeeze the juice. Add to plums in pot.

3. Stir in raisins and sugar.

4. Cook over medium heat, stirring, until mixture begins to bubble.

5. Turn heat down until mixture simmers (bubbles slowly around edges).

6. Stir mixture occasionally to keep it from sticking. Cook 45 minutes to one hour or until mixture is thick.

7. Add chopped nuts. Remove from heat and cool.

8. Store in refrigerator or freezer.

*Grate only the colored part of the peel, not the white part underneath.

Note: All recipes should be prepared with adult supervision.

Mrs. Twiggenbotham's Lemon Blueberry Tea Bread
Makes one lovely loaf

3 cups flour
3 teaspoons baking powder
½ teaspoon baking soda
1 teaspoon salt
grated rind of two lemons*
¼ cup soft butter
¾ cup sugar

1 large egg
1 cup milk
½ cup fresh lemon juice
(about 2 lemons)
1 cup fresh blueberries (or frozen
ones that have been partially thawed)

1. Preheat oven to 350 degrees. Spray a 9x5x3 inch loaf pan with non-stick spray. Set aside.

2. In a large bowl, mix the flour, baking powder, baking soda, salt, and lemon rind. Set aside.

3. In mixer, on medium speed, cream butter and sugar until light and fluffy.

4. Beat in the egg.

5. With mixer on low speed, add some of the flour mixture to creamed mixture. Then add some milk. Then add some lemon juice. Repeat until all ingredients, except blueberries, are mixed in.

6. Gently fold blueberries into batter.

7. Spread batter in loaf pan. Bake for 60–65 minutes, or until a toothpick inserted into the center of the loaf comes out clean.

8. Cool in pan for 5 minutes. Turn out onto a cooling rack and cool completely. Wrap in plastic wrap to keep tea bread fresh.

*Grate only the colored part of the peel, not the white part underneath.